Impeachment Chronicle

Constituent Letters

Impeachment Chronicle

Constituent Letters

By H. C. Hallett

Blue Roan Press

Copyright © 2020 Blue Roan Press
All rights reserved.
ISBN: 978-0-578-75350-8
Library of Congress Control Number: 2020916416

First Edition 2020

Blue Roan Press
Waukesha, Wisconsin
www.aquaartideas.com

About the Cover Art

The cover of this book features a painting by the author, "Travels with a Donkey: Best Way Forward," oil on book cover, 6.5" x 4." It is one of a series painted onto the covers of a collection of books by Robert Louis Stevenson (1850-1894). The collection was published in 1925 by Charles Scribner's Sons.

The series of paintings is called *Progressions* and can be seen on the back cover of this book. The cover paintings are inspired by the title of each RLS book and relate to current issues in the 21st century. Other painting titles in the series include "Treasure Island," "Dr. Jekyll and Mr. Hyde: Outside appearance shouldn't matter, but it does," "In the South Seas: Effects of Climate Change," "New Arabian Nights," and "Letters: Connections of Old." The *Progressions* series repurposes 19th century titles to focus attention on issues of today. To see more of the author's work, please visit www.aquaartideas.com.

Dedicated with gratitude to
the tireless journalists at
the Milwaukee Journal Sentinel,
TIME Magazine, and
National Public Radio

Contents

Introduction	1
Chapter 1 – House Impeachment	3
Chapter 2 – Senate Trial	19
Aftermath	43
Glossary of Personnel	46

Introduction

I didn't save my first letter. It was likely a short note letting my representative in Congress know that I supported the House of Representatives' impeachment inquiry. I live in a gerrymandered district in Wisconsin, and it is frustrating to repeatedly have my views on certain issues go unrepresented in Congress. I think it's important for our elected officials to listen to all of their constituents, and I wanted my representative, Jim Sensenbrenner, to know he did indeed have constituents that stood in support of the impeachment process. The following letter at the beginning of Chapter 1 is his reply. I did start to save my letters after that, primarily so I could keep track of what I had just said as well as a means of following the proceedings. I respectfully signed my letters with my first and last name and submitted them to my U.S. Congress members through their official websites. I started to write to Senator Ron Johnson when it was reported in the news that the Republican-controlled Senate planned to quickly acquit an impeached President Trump before ever even holding a real trial.

In summary, the issue at hand involved the impeachment of President Trump for abuse of power and obstruction of Congress due to his illegal withholding of congressionally mandated military assistance funds and a promised White House meeting from

Ukraine's President Zelensky in exchange for Zelensky conducting investigations into the presumptive Democratic presidential nominee, Joe Biden, and his son, Hunter. Obstruction of Congress occurred when Trump ordered government officials not to comply with the House Intelligence Committee's subpoenas and requests for relevant documents and testimony.

There were so many false statements from the beginning that my objective became to keep the truth in focus. Lest we forget, it's chronicled here.

Chapter 1
House Impeachment

October 21, 2019

Dear Dr. Hallett:

Thank you for contacting me with your support for impeaching President Trump. I appreciate hearing from you.

I understand you are concerned with the whistleblower's report that alleges misconduct occurred in a phone call between President Trump and the newly elected Ukrainian President. We now know the contents of the actual phone call thanks to the Administration's decision to release the transcripts of the conversation. I read the transcripts and do not believe they show any impeachable activity by the President.

If Speaker Pelosi is serious about beginning an impeachment inquiry, then the House must formally vote to authorize it. Without a formal vote, President Trump will continue to be subject to partisan attacks by Democrat-led House committees and denied his constitutional right of due process.

While I realize we may disagree on this issue, please know I respect your views. Thank you again for contacting me.

Sincerely,

F. JAMES SENSENBRENNER, JR.
Member of Congress

10-25-19

Dear Representative Sensenbrenner,

    The House is not required to vote on an impeachment inquiry authorization. There is very legitimate concern that impeachable offenses have been committed, and the purpose of the inquiry is to look into those concerns to see if there are grounds for impeachment, and if so, then the House votes on whether or not to impeach the president (simple majority needed). The House and Speaker Pelosi are following procedural precedent. In the past, Congress has identified three general categories that constitute grounds for impeachment: "1) Improperly exceeding or abusing the powers of the office, 2) Behavior incompatible with the function and purpose of the office, and 3) Misusing the office for an improper purpose or for personal gain." While you may feel the phone call in question doesn't raise concern, there are others who feel that it does fall into some of these categories. The purpose of the inquiry is to sort this out. The inquiry is being conducted in a transparent manner with evidence and findings being made public as the inquiry committee conducts its investigation. Once the inquiry is complete, then the decision is made whether or not to vote formally for impeachment.

If the president is impeached by the House, then the Senate tries the accused with the Chief Justice of the U.S. presiding. The Senate determines with a vote whether or not to convict the impeached president. The president has not in the least been denied this "due process," nor is there any intention of denying it in the future if impeachment occurs. If the impeached president is convicted (2/3 super majority vote required for conviction), then the impeached president would be removed from office.
Sincerely,

(exact date not recorded)

Dear Representative Sensenbrenner,

The House has approved a public phase of the impeachment inquiry which is what the Republicans wanted, and as a member of Congress, it is your job and responsibility to participate in the process honestly. House Republicans are attempting to confuse the public, question the legitimacy of the witnesses, and promote already dis-proven conspiracy theories, all to protect Trump.

The Republican Party has sold its soul for power. As your constituent, I urge you put country above Party, and put your oath to the Constitution above personal loyalty to Donald Trump.

When are Republicans going to admit that they backed the wrong man? History will look favorably on any Republican who stands against Trump's abuses of power.
Sincerely,

November 5, 2019

Dear Dr. Hallett:

Thank you for contacting me regarding your view that Trump Administration officials should be held in contempt. I appreciate hearing from you.

I believe that an effort to hold these officials in contempt would be overtly political and unnecessarily divisive. Our country is facing a number of pressing issues like the opioid crisis, the situation on our southern border, and mounting pressures from China on trade and theft of intellectual property. It is my hope that the House of Representatives focuses its energy on coming up with real solutions to the issues that are affecting everyday Americans, as opposed to issues that are politically driven and partisan in nature.

I know that we disagree on this issue, but please know that I respect your opinion. Thanks again for contacting me.

Sincerely,

F. JAMES SENSENBRENNER, JR.
Member of Congress

11-5-19

Dear Representative Sensenbrenner,

    Thanks for responding. It seems that the House could function much more efficiently without the obstruction tactics.
    If you're going to tackle pressing issues, I want you to know that I wholeheartedly support gun control. I support expanded,

universal background checks, red flag laws, and bans on assault weapons and all of their various accouterments.

I think it's alright for people to have rifles for hunting and/or target shooting sports, and I think those weapons should be made as "smart" as possible with the latest technology that we have available.

Sincerely,

11-16-19

Dear Representative Sensenbrenner,

Please support the impeachment of a president that has abused the powers of office time and again (obstruction of justice, trying to discredit and tamper with witnesses, using the office for personal gain, etc.). History will look favorably on any Republican who stands up against Trump's abuse of the presidency. Do you really want the legacy of your long and illustrious career to be defined by being a stooge to Trump?

Please listen to the facts and their repercussions that are being presented to you during the hearings and see them without the Republican Party "spin."

Sincerely,

11-17-19

Dear Representative Sensenbrennner,

Please support impeachment. President Trump is a liar. From day 1 of his presidency, he has distorted facts to benefit himself, and he continues to do so to this day. Trump only released aid to Ukraine and only made assertions denying a quid pro quo once he was advised that things were "getting too hot under the collar." Please listen to the statements being presented to you during the hearing and hear them honestly without the Republican Party's "spin."

It would be a shame for the legacy of your long and distinguished career to be defined by your actions of being a stooge to Trump.

Sincerely,

11-20-19

Dear Representative Sensenbrenner,

Please support the impeachment of President Trump. Trying to discredit the witnesses presenting statements during the congressional hearings is absolutely ridiculous. These are career State Department officials or military officers who understand their duty and responsibility toward their country, and who were appropriately alarmed by the abuses of power that they witnessed.

In your Republican circle, discrediting the witness has been an effective defense strategy in the past with sexual assault accusations. It has worked well for you all when there is one main witness, and it comes down to the testimony of "he said versus she said." That modus operandi won't work in this situation with Ukraine. There are simply too many 1st-hand witnesses saying the same thing. I'm pretty sure Ambassador Sondland's* attorney told him he better tell the truth, or he will go to jail. He is following that advice and telling the truth under oath. It's very easy for those not under oath to issue disparaging statements against him, and it's your job to sort through those smokescreens. President Zelensky's statement has been tossed around as another smokescreen, but his is the weakest "evidence" of all because he believes his financial aid is dependent on Trump's favor. Ergo, of course he will say that he didn't feel pressured. I'd like someone to ask him if he was going to instigate any of the requested investigations and then watch him pause for a bit to try to figure out the best way to answer that question, but that's just speculation. The real evidence is being presented to you during the hearings. Please listen to what the witnesses under oath are saying and hear them honestly without the Republican Party's distortions.

    You are not even running for re-election. Now is your chance to separate yourself from those that have sold their souls for power and stand up for what is right for the country. Don't let your legacy be defined by being a stooge to Trump.

Sincerely,

*See Glossary of Personnel p. 46

                                                                                            11-23-19

Dear Representative Sensenbrenner,

    Please support the impeachment of President Trump. The Republican Party needs to move forward without the demagoguery of Trump. In addition to the obvious, substantiated abuses of power in the current Ukraine case, Trump has relied on the incitement of violence and prejudice, the spreading of lies, bullying tactics, and obstruction of justice to benefit himself and promote his belief that the world shouldn't change because he was able to make a lot of money in the current system. The "business acumen" that he has brought to government doesn't care about the environment, civil rights, responsible foreign policy, or making our country or the world a better place for everyone. Trump will also turn against any Republican who stands up to his abuses.

    I'm not sure if you're seeing my constituent letters. You can just reply, "Thanks, I've read your letter," since I know you are very busy during these impeachment proceedings, and your vote on impeachment will tell me whether you've been swayed by what has been presented to you or not. Again, don't let the legacy of

your long and distinguished career be defined by being a stooge to Trump. The Republican Party can do better than this.
Sincerely,

11-26-19

Dear Representative Sensenbrenner,

  Please support the impeachment of President Trump. The Republican Party has covered for him for far too long. The involvement of Nunes, the lead Republican on the House Intelligence Committee conducting the impeachment hearings, in the Ukraine situation he is supposed to be investigating has come to light. Seriously, how can you continue to pretend this is even remotely acceptable?

  You may think that your vote doesn't matter because there are enough Democrats in the House now to vote for impeachment, and you don't have to "compromise" yourself. I would put forth that not supporting impeachment given all of the evidence we have heard is an even more compromising position. Your vote in support of impeachment will send a message to your colleagues in the Senate that it is time to end the cover-up. The Republican Party appears to be corrupt on this through and through. Please have the courage to stand up for what is right and to stand against Trump. Don't be complicit in his abuses of power, coercion, corruption, obstruction, bribery, prevarication, and slander. Separate yourself from the Republicans who have sold their souls for power and vote to support impeachment.
Sincerely,

12-2-19

Dear Representative Sensenbrenner,

Please vote in support of impeachment. From what I've heard, the testimony during the hearings confirmed Trump's abuses of the power of the presidency. Please listen honestly to what the witnesses have said and hear them without the Republican Party's distortions. Trump is refusing to believe the analysis of foreign influence presented by our own highly qualified and knowledgeable intelligence professionals. His irresponsible, irreparable "foreign policy" is downright dangerous for our country and for many others. Please don't be complicit in his dealings.

The Republican Party could be so much better than Trump. Please have the courage to stand up for what is right. Don't let the legacy of your long and distinguished career be defined by being a stooge to Trump. Support impeachment and show your colleagues that an upstanding path forward is possible.

Sincerely,

12-2-19

Dear Senator Johnson,

If President Trump is impeached, please consider supporting conviction. From what I've heard, the testimony during the impeachment hearings confirmed Trump's abuses of the power of his office. Please listen honestly to what the witnesses have said and hear them without the Republican Party's distortions and "spin." Trump is refusing to believe the analysis of foreign influence presented by our own highly qualified and knowledgeable intelligence professionals. His irresponsible, irreparable "foreign policy" is downright dangerous for our country and for many others. Please don't be complicit in his dealings.

The Republican Party could be so much better than Trump. Please have the courage to stand up for what is right. Don't let the legacy of your long and distinguished career be defined by being a stooge to Trump. If a Senate trial comes to pass, I urge you to listen to the facts presented and show your colleagues that an upstanding path forward is possible.
Sincerely,

12-8-19

Dear Representative Sensenbrenner,
   Please vote in favor of impeaching President Trump. Testimony from legal experts has now confirmed that his abuses of power are impeachable offenses. When will the Republican Party admit that they hitched their cart to the wrong horse? Those defending Trump have sold their souls for power that isn't going to last. History will look favorably on anyone who stands up against Trump and his obstructions and lies.
   Trump has alienated so many people and is incapable of governing for the future. Show the GOP that the best way forward is without him and guide your Party out of this morass. Let your legacy be one of courage. The Republicans have backed the wrong horse; please support impeachment.
Sincerely,

12-8-19

Dear Senator Johnson,
   Please vote in favor of convicting President Trump should impeachment come to pass. Testimony from legal experts has now confirmed that his abuses of power are impeachable offenses. President Trump is a liar. From day 1 of his presidency, he has

distorted facts to benefit himself, and he continues to do so to this day. Trump only released aid to Ukraine and only made assertions denying a quid pro quo once he was advised that things were "getting too hot under the collar." You must realize that he lied to you when you asked him point blank if there was a quid pro quo involved.

When will the Republican Party admit that they hitched their cart to the wrong horse? Those defending Trump have sold their souls for power that isn't going to last. History will look favorably on anyone who stands up against Trump and his obstructions and lies. Trump has alienated so many people and is incapable of governing for the future. Show the GOP that the best way forward is without him and guide your Party out of this morass. Let your legacy be one of courage. The Republicans have backed the wrong horse; please support conviction.
Sincerely,

12-13-19

Dear Senator Baldwin,
    I'm just letting you know that I fully support the impeachment and conviction of President Trump for abusing the powers of office and obstruction. Thank you for standing by our Constitution.
Sincerely,

12-13-19: The House Judiciary Committee voted on articles of impeachment adopting abuse of power and obstruction of Congress. Votes were strictly along party lines 23-17 including Representative Sensenbrenner (R-WI) voting against.

12-14-19

Dear Representative Sensenbrenner,
    Please vote for the impeachment of President Trump for abuse of power and obstruction of Congress. The witness testimony from seasoned State Department officials and a military officer (Lt. Col. Vindman) who all understand their responsibility to their country has been quite clear. They recognized and were appropriately alarmed by the president's use of his office for personal political gain and his initial attempts to hide the full contents and import of his July 25th call with Ukraine's President Zelensky. The bottom line is that Trump used his office to solicit maneuvers intended to damage the election prospects of one of his political opponents which constitutes an abuse of power. He then further proceeded to tell government officials not to comply with congressional subpoenas, a blatant act of obstruction.
    Don't lose sight of the honest witness testimony as the Republican Party continues to distract and distort the issues to defend their "house of cards." The White House is taking bits and pieces of the testimony or focusing on only part of a narrative to try to twist the context. For instance, they say the president is allowed to set policy. Yes, but he's not allowed to set policy for personal gain.
    A common GOP evasion technique is to ask, "Why not wait for the upcoming election?" In answer, there are two major reasons not to wait for the election: 1) Trump is abusing his powers of office to influence that very election in his favor and consequently sabotaging our democratic election process. 2) He had put our country in a potentially dangerous and exploitable position, was willing to undermine essential strategic foreign policy for his personal political benefit, seems not to understand the risks involved, and therefore wouldn't hesitate to do it again. These are exactly the type of executive branch offenses you swore

to safeguard our country from when you took an oath to support and protect our Constitution.

    The Republicans defending Trump are gambling on fallacies to prop him up. They would be in a much better position in the long run if they banked on the truth and moved forward without Trump. Please show courageous leadership and vote for impeachment.
Sincerely,

12-17-19

Support Removal from Office; Here's Why

Dear Senator Johnson,
    Please vote for the conviction of an impeached President Trump for abuse of power and obstruction of Congress. The witness testimony from seasoned State Department officials and a military officer (Lt. Col. Vindman) who all understand their responsibility to their country has been quite clear. They recognized and were appropriately alarmed by the president's use of his office for personal political gain and his initial attempts to hide the full contents and import of the July 25th call. The bottom line is that Trump used his office to solicit maneuvers intended to damage the election prospects of one of his political opponents which constitutes an abuse of power. He then further proceeded to tell government officials not to comply with congressional subpoenas, a blatant act of obstruction.
    Don't lose sight of the honest witness testimony as the Republican Party continues to distract and distort the issues to defend their "house of cards." The White House is taking bits and pieces of the testimony or focusing on only part of a narrative to try to twist the context. For instance, they say the president is allowed to set policy. Yes, but he's not allowed to set policy for personal gain.

A common GOP evasion technique is to ask, "Why not wait for the upcoming election?" In answer, there are two major reasons not to wait for the election: 1) Trump is abusing his powers of office to influence that very election in his favor and consequently sabotaging our democratic election process. 2) He had put our country in a potentially dangerous and exploitable position, was willing to undermine essential strategic foreign policy for his personal political benefit, seems not to understand the risks involved, and therefore wouldn't hesitate to do it again. These are exactly the type of executive branch offenses you swore to safeguard our country from when you took an oath to support and protect our Constitution.

The Republicans defending Trump are gambling on fallacies to prop him up. They would be in a much better position in the long run if they banked on the truth and moved forward without Trump. Please show courageous leadership and vote for conviction.
Sincerely,

12-17-19

Dear Representative Sensenbrenner,

Please vote for the impeachment of President Trump for abusing the powers of office and obstruction of Congress. Take a step away from your partisan political defenses and see Trump's actions and motives clearly. His motives are self-serving above all else: above the good of our country, above our Constitution, and above the law. Rudy Giuliani has just stated again that he and Trump forced out the U.S. Ambassador to Ukraine Marie Yovanovitch because she was going to make it difficult to get the investigations into the Bidens underway. You have her testimony from the impeachment hearings. She recognized the changes in the congressional Ukraine policy being made by President Trump

for his own political gain and recognized all of their ramifications to U.S. national security of which Trump continues to be ignorant. The Republican Party could be so much better than this. Let the legacy of your long and distinguished career be defined by a courageously principled stance. Vote in favor of impeachment tomorrow.
With the utmost sincerity,

12-18-19: The U.S. House of Representatives voted 230-197 to approve the first article of impeachment charging Trump with abuse of power. The second article of impeachment charging Trump with obstruction of Congress was approved 229-198. Trump became the third president to be impeached in U.S. history. Representative Sensenbrenner (R-WI) voted against impeachment.
    Andrew Johnson was impeached in 1868 and Bill Clinton in 1998. Richard Nixon resigned in 1974 before he could be impeached.

12-19-19

Dear Representative Sensenbrenner,
    In listening to some of yesterday's impeachment debate, I heard the Republicans as a whole ignore the evidence implicating Trump and instead try to drown it out by repeatedly referencing a tangential claim that the Democratic representatives have been trying to override the results of the 2016 elections. There are gaping holes in that narrative. You don't seem to believe it, but the Democrats came to Congress to help craft a government that worked for the American people. Your narrative conveniently leaves out the 2018 midterm election results where the people

chose to elect enough representatives in the House to put a check on Trump. The ability of the House to impeach Trump is the will of the people, and Trump gave them the reason with his shenanigans in dealing with Ukraine.

    Needless to say, your vote against impeachment was extraordinarily disappointing.

Sincerely,

Chapter 2
Senate Trial

12-19-19

Dear Senator Johnson,
    Please support the conviction of impeached President Trump for abusing the powers of office and obstruction of Congress. I am appealing to your sense of justice now because it is uncertain what kind of trial will be conducted, and you have overwhelming evidence in front of you already. Take a step away from your partisan political defenses and see Trump's actions and motives clearly. His motives are self-serving above all else: above the good of our country, above our Constitution, and above the law.
    Rudy Giuliani has recently stated again that he and Trump forced out the U.S. Ambassador to Ukraine Marie Yovanovitch because she was going to make it difficult to get the investigations into the Bidens underway. You have her testimony from the impeachment hearings. She recognized the changes in the congressional Ukraine policy being made by President Trump for his own political gain and recognized all of their ramifications to U.S. national security of which Trump continues to be ignorant.

The Republican Party could be so much better than this. Let the legacy of your long and distinguished career be defined by a courageously principled stance. If Republican Senators want to act like the trial is a done deal, then I will urge you now to vote in favor of conviction.
With the utmost sincerity,

12-20-19
Dear Senators Johnson and Baldwin,
    I'm a constituent who doesn't want a farce for an impeachment trial. A trial to remove Donald Trump from the presidency is a serious matter. All of the evidence must be presented and witnesses brought in to testify. If the Senate does not hold a fair trial, it will appear as a cover-up. Americans deserve a full, fair, and transparent impeachment trial.
Sincerely,

12-21-19
Dear Senator Johnson,
    The House Judiciary Committee meticulously conducted an impeachment inquiry gathering transcripts and testimony as accurately as possible with Trump trying to thwart and disrupt the proceedings at every turn. Now Republican senators are saying they will sweep all of the evidence under the rug and attempt to protect Trump with a charade for a trial. This pretense is a cover-up.
    In listening to some of the House's impeachment debate, I heard the Republicans as a whole ignore the evidence implicating Trump and instead try to drown it out by repeatedly referencing a

tangential claim that the Democratic representatives have been trying to override the results of the 2016 election. There are gaping holes in that narrative. You don't seem to believe it, but the Democrats came to Congress to help craft a government that worked for the American people. Your narrative conveniently leaves out the 2018 midterm election results where the people chose to elect enough representatives in the House to put a check on Trump. The ability of the House to impeach Trump is the will of the people, and Trump gave them the reason with his shenanigans in dealing with Ukraine.
    Stop covering for Trump. The Republican Party would be better off to move forward without him. He has compromised your integrity.
Sincerely,

12-29-19
Dear Senator Johnson,
    The intelligence analyst who became the whistleblower by alerting Congress of President Trump's corrupt dealings with Ukraine first tried to report to the Office of the Inspector General. The inspector general found the report credible, but those higher up in the intelligence community were being told by the White House to block the inspector general from sending the report to Congress. There was a Republican realization of corruption and attempted cover-up from the very beginning.
    In a situation of presidential corruption, it is the duty of Congress to check the president abusing his powers of office. Yet Senate Majority Leader McConnell has come out and said he won't be an impartial juror, and he will coordinate the "trial" of the impeached president with the president's White House counsel by conducting a "trial" without witness testimony or the presentation of evidence for review. Republican Senator Graham, chairman of

the Senate Judiciary Committee has also said he intends to have a quick "trial" and will not even try to pretend to be a fair juror.

A lot of accusations of partisanship have been flying around, but you really can't get more partisan than refusing to acknowledge the solid evidence behind the impeachment of Trump. There are transcripts of Trump implicating himself. There is witness testimony from multiple quarters: former and current U.S. ambassadors to Ukraine, former and current National Security Council senior directors for Europe and Russia, a National Security Council director for European Affairs, the U.S. ambassador to the European Union, a special advisor to the vice president for Europe and Russia, a counselor for Political Affairs at the U.S. Embassy in Ukraine; the list goes on.

Again, there is sound, direct evidence backing up the impeachment vote and those covering for Trump have lost their integrity and credibility. Don't be complicit in his dealings. The Republican Party has backed the wrong horse and would be better served in the long run to have Pence finish out the term until the 2020 elections. History will respect the witnesses who testified and anyone who stood up for what is right during these proceedings. Please advocate for a fair trial with witness testimony and evidential documents.
Sincerely,

1-3-20

Dear Senator Johnson,

Senators covering for Trump look like foolish pawns when they ignore and deny evidence of abuse of power that the general public can see quite clearly. As the abuses occurred, numerous reports were made to the National Security Council's (NSC) law department to alert them of Trump's illicit dealings.

When then National Security Advisor John Bolton heard of Trump wanting the Ukrainians to launch investigations into a political rival and the conditional nature of those investigations, it seems Bolton recognized the danger posed to our national security along with Trump's use of his office for personal political gain, and he instructed NSC Senior Director Fiona Hill to tell one of the NSC's lead lawyers, John Eisenberg, that he (Bolton) was not part of the scheme, according to Hill's testimony during the House impeachment hearings.

In separate instances, NSC Director Lt. Col. Vindman also notified Eisenberg twice about his concerns with what he had seen of Trump's Ukraine dealings, and according to Vindman's testimony, Eisenberg came back to him shortly thereafter and told him not to discuss the situation with anyone else. It has been reported that Eisenberg did meet with Trump and White House Counsel Pat Cipollone, who by then had heard of the whistleblower's concerns, but it appears that Trump was unable to comprehend the implications of or the seriousness of the actions he took involving Ukraine.

Trump's irresponsible, irreparable "foreign policy" is downright dangerous for our country and for many others. Trump has warped your service to your country into a dysfunctional service/worship of his demagoguery. Please have the courage to separate yourself and the Republican Party from Trump and stand up for what is right.
Sincerely,

1-6-20
Against War/For Conviction of Impeached President Trump:
Dear Senators Johnson and Baldwin, and Representative Sensenbrenner,

    In case you are distracted by Trump's killing of Iran's Major General Qasem Soleimani which wasn't authorized by Congress or discussed with the Joint Chiefs of Staff, I want to bring to your attention recent new evidence pertaining to the impeachment trial. Unredacted emails have now been released unequivocally showing that it was Trump who ordered the 84-day hold on military assistance dollars to Ukraine as part of a quid pro quo and that numerous staff members at the Pentagon, Office of Management and Budget (OMB), and the White House, realizing the illegality of not complying with Congress' allocation, were scrambling to find ways to make it "sound legal." The documents were previously only available from the Trump administration in redacted form (obstruction).

    It's extremely unfortunate that Trump wasn't removed peaceably from office through our Constitution's channels before he could assassinate Soleimani, the commander of Iran's Islamic Revolutionary Guard Corps' Quds Force. What will the quid pro quo for that be? For the record, I think war is archaic, and there has to be a better way.

    "An eye for an eye makes the whole world blind." - Mahatma Gandhi

Sincerely,

TAMMY BALDWIN
WISCONSIN

United States Senate
WASHINGTON, DC 20510

1-10-20

COMMITTEES:
APPROPRIATIONS
COMMERCE
HEALTH, EDUCATION,
LABOR, AND PENSIONS

Dear Dr. Hallett:

Thank you for contacting me about the impeachment of President Donald Trump. I appreciate hearing from you.

On December 18, 2019, the House of Representatives voted to impeach President Trump for abuse of power and obstruction of Congress. I understand that people have different opinions about President Trump's actions. I believe that we must have a fair and honest bipartisan impeachment trial in the Senate that allows each side to make its case.

I support the release of critical documents and calling witnesses that have firsthand knowledge about President Trump's actions, including his withholding of a promised White House meeting with Ukraine's President and congressionally mandated U.S. military aid to help Ukraine fight Russian aggression, in an attempt to deliver personal, political benefits to himself.

It is wrong that the President has issued an Administration-wide directive to defy all subpoenas related to the House impeachment inquiry of these actions, just as it is wrong for Senate Majority Leader McConnell to prevent witnesses from testifying. Former National Security Advisor John Bolton, Acting Chief of Staff Mick Mulvaney, and senior White House aides Robert Blair and Michael Duffey can provide direct, first-hand evidence, under oath, about the President's actions, and they should appear as witnesses in a Senate impeachment trial so we have all the facts and evidence.

As your Senator, I took an oath of office to support and defend the Constitution. In a Senate impeachment trial, every Senator will take an oath to do impartial justice. I take this responsibility very seriously and my judgment on the charges that President Trump abused his power for personal, political gain and obstructed Congress will be guided by my constitutional duty to put country before party, because no one in America, including our President, is above the rule of law.

Once again, thank you for contacting my office. It is important for me to hear from the people of Wisconsin on the issues, thoughts and concerns that matter most to you. If I can be of further assistance, please visit my website at www.baldwin.senate.gov for information on how to contact my office.
   Sincerely,

Tammy Baldwin
United States Senator

                                                1-11-20
Dear Senator Johnson,
   You have miscalculated the support for Trump. I can only assume that you continue to back him and ignore evidence of his corruption because you think it is the best way to maintain your power. Don't be blinded by that power. Many, many people that voted for Trump initially were misled, and while they don't like to admit it, they are figuring it out daily. Trump's reliance on deceit and intimidation to make himself seem influential will not last as you presume.

By his own admission, Senate Majority Leader McConnell won't conduct a fair trial on the articles of impeachment. McConnell has lost his credibility and is no longer trusted. Hence House Speaker Pelosi's withholding of the impeachment articles until McConnell confirms in writing that witnesses will be permitted to give testimony during the trial. This is not an unreasonable request and is, in fact, the actual framework for conducting a trial. According to the United States Department of Justice's website under Justice 101, "The trial is a structured process where the facts of a case are presented to a jury, and they decide if the defendant is guilty or not guilty of the charge offered. During trial, the prosecutor uses witnesses and evidence to prove to the jury that the defendant committed the crime(s). The defendant, represented by an attorney, also tells his side of the story using witnesses and evidence." In this case where the Senate is the jury, it's your obligation to have a complete trial and not a sham.

You are in a position where you can persuade your Senate colleagues to conduct a fair trial and restore the public's confidence in the Senate. All it would take is the courage to see the truth and the writing on the wall.

Sincerely,

January 14, 2020

Dear Dr. Hallett:

Thank you for contacting me with your concerns over increasing tensions with Iran. I appreciate hearing from you.

I am supportive of the President's decisive actions to take out Iranian General Qasem Soleimani. General Soleimani was responsible for countless attacks, both military and terroristic in nature, across the Middle East. He commanded Iran's Quds Force, which was responsible for training and arming militias operating in Syria, Iraq, Yemen, and other conflict areas in the region.

Our intelligence agencies have concluded that General Soleimani was directly responsible for the death of at least 600 Americans and for thousands more across the world. I applaud the President for showing that there are consequences for attacking Americans and American installations, like our embassy in Baghdad.

Rest assured that as a member of the House Foreign Affairs Committee I will continue to monitor any developments.

Thanks again for contacting me.

Sincerely,

F. James Sensenbrenner, Jr.

F. JAMES SENSENBRENNER, JR.
Member of Congress

1-14-20

Dear Senator Johnson,

 Former National Security Advisor John Bolton has said he would comply with a subpoena to testify during the impeachment trial, but now Trump is saying he won't let that happen. A defendant doesn't prevent a witness from testifying unless the trial is "fixed." Why wouldn't Trump want Bolton to testify? Fear of incrimination perhaps?

 Trump has a pattern of trying to keep things from public view (his tax returns, the Mueller Report, hush money payments, various obstruction gambits, etc.). Wouldn't it be nice to work with someone that you didn't have to cover for all of the time? Instead

of looking united, Republican senators appear vacuous and unable to think for themselves. Please conduct a true trial and look at the evidence honestly. The Republican Party has the chance to move forward with a different leader. Someone more competent and able to govern responsibly without corruption would be a good place to start.
Sincerely,

1-17-20
Dear Senator Johnson,
    President Trump came to Wisconsin and did the old fear-mongering thing again. I find it to be the hallmark of a stale politician who has no coherent vision for the future and no consideration for what the future might bring. There are numerous examples of this with Trump: failing to acknowledge climate change, not realizing the compounding effects of tariffs on already struggling farmers, rash foreign policy decisions/reversals, just to name a few. But I digress.
    The articles of impeachment are now in the Senate's hands, and I've been pleading with you to conduct a fair trial with witness testimony and evidence. New evidence continues to come forth. We now have papers from Lev Parnas who was working with Giuliani in Ukraine. These papers give further details on the White House's plan to have Ambassador Yovanovitch removed from her post for not cooperating with their illegal scheme to influence the 2020 elections. Parnas is also saying that Trump knew all about it as it was happening and that Bolton would be the reliable witness that you've been looking for who could corroborate a lot of the claims being made.

Please evaluate all of the evidence. In this trial, you are under oath to consider evidence within a legal context and not in a distorted manner that serves someone's "best interest."
Sincerely,

1-20-20

Dear Senator Johnson,
    I know you're aware of the nonpartisan Government Accountability Office report that recently came out. It found that Trump's Office of Management and Budget (OMB) broke the law by withholding $391 million in security assistance from Ukraine, assistance that was specifically earmarked by Congress for Ukraine. The people at the OMB are not criminals. They were acting on Trump's orders and tried to let the White House know the orders were in violation of the Impoundment Control Act.
    I also notice you're saying you never had contact with Lev Parnas and are suspicious of his timing (1) as if these are reasons why you want to dismiss his documents. Well, of course you didn't have contact with him. The whole point is that Trump was bypassing Congress (you) with his own back channels to use the powers of his office for personal political gain, the abuse of power addressed in the 1st article of impeachment you're supposed to be considering. Are you trying to say you weren't involved with the back channels? As for the timing, Parnas was subpoenaed by the House Intelligence Committee on October 10th. The subpoena was ignored because of orders from Trump not to comply, part of the obstruction tactics addressed in the 2nd article of impeachment you're supposed to be considering.
    I'm trying to tell you that the evidence against Trump is overwhelming. Even from the House inquiry alone, it is quite clear. The general public can see it. McConnell appears as a conniving accomplice with all of his shenanigans from trying to hold a sham trial to restricting access by the press. Don't be

complicit in the cover-up any longer. Cut your losses, finish out the term with Pence, and put up a Republican candidate who isn't tainted by corruption for the 2020 elections.

In cases like this, history eventually reveals and remembers the truth, while the conspiracy theories and conspiracists are proven wrong. Which side do you want your legacy to be on?

Sincerely,

1) Milwaukee Journal Sentinel, "Baldwin, Johnson view trial differently" by Craig Gilbert, pp. 1A and 12A; 1-19-20.

1-23-20

Dear Senator Johnson,

I have been listening to some of the live broadcast of the impeachment trial. Intelligence Committee Chair Adam Schiff and the rest of the House management team are laying out the entire case for you with substantial evidence right in front of your eyes, and it is rock solid. I can see President Trump's involvement in and orchestration of the scheme to influence the 2020 elections in his favor, the quid pro quo, the national security implications, the bypassing of Congress and seasoned diplomatic channels, the coercion of staff to act illegally, the solicitation of foreign influence on our elections, and the attempts to hide and stifle evidence which are being abetted by congressional Republicans. Trump's defense team is evading the truth and hasn't produced a shred of evidence to support their statements. I can see it. The whole country can see it. How you can sit there and turn a blind eye is beyond the pale. What can you possibly hope to gain by condoning Trump's actions?

I'm still hearing Republican senators willfully ignoring key details to conform to their party line narrative, so here's a review to clarify. When Biden was vice president, he was acting on instructions from Congress and the State Department to help remove a Ukrainian official from office who was internationally known for corruption. In contrast, it's not okay for a president to bypass Congress to solicit a foreign government to investigate a political rival. Another misleading partial narrative is that a president is allowed to replace an ambassador. You are conveniently leaving out that it's not okay for Trump to remove an ambassador (Yovanovitch) because they were standing in the way of his quid pro quo exchange of security assistance and a White House meeting for launching investigations into his political rival. The public doesn't like to be tricked by lies and half-truths.

Make no mistake. If you fail to convict Trump in this trial, you are defending, condoning, and abetting the abuse of power and the obstruction of justice.

Sincerely,

1-24-20

Dear Senator Johnson,

Why did Russia start hacking into Burisma's files back in November? Probably because they knew their Trump puppet was in trouble, and they're looking for any snippet ideally involving the Bidens that they can take out of context or twist slightly and magnify on the internet to mislead as many people as possible during the impeachment process or before the elections. After all, it worked last time, so now they're going to do it again.

I've heard that many Republican senators are leaving the room for long periods of time during the impeachment trial case presentations which they're not supposed to do. Do they then plan

to say they didn't hear any compelling evidence (because they weren't in the room)? Are you proud? Are Republican senators proud to be gaming the system? Do you think you're smarter and better than all Democrats and Independents? Are you proud to be defending Trump puppet?
Sincerely,

1-26-20
Dear Senator Johnson,
    I heard portions of the Trump defense team's arguments yesterday, and while I always suspected it, I can see pretty clearly now why you're so adamant about not convicting an impeached president. I heard the defense essentially talking directly to the Republican senators and loudly asking them if they wanted to change all of the ballots for the 2020 election. They weren't trying to convince the general public of any innocence. Threatening an imminent ballot change is not a defense of the impeachable offenses. Instead, they were fear-mongering. Their implied meaning to the Republican senators was that they would lose their power and possibly their jobs if they put someone other than Trump on the ballot. A jury making decisions based on fear instead of searching for the truth will refuse to hear or believe any of the evidence presented to them.
    I know the Republican Party has people who are highly qualified to run for office and not tainted by corruption. I've said from the beginning that you've hitched your cart to the wrong horse. Now's your chance to put up a candidate who isn't corrupt or impeached. It's actually very sound advice. It could even be called nonpartisan advice.
Sincerely,

1-29-20

Dear Senator Johnson,
    It's time to move on from the Trump defense team's smear campaign against Biden, which by the way, is not a refutation of Trump's abuse of power, nor does it excuse that abuse even if the smears were true. (Nepotism in the private sector is not illegal as long as potential conflicts of interest are disclosed to shareholders and there is no discrimination going on.)
    I'd like to move on to your next crisis which is Bolton's book manuscript being released to the public and stating that Trump told Bolton directly that military aid to Ukraine was being withheld until Ukraine investigated Trump's political rival. It confirms that Bolton is that firsthand witness you've been looking for. Hearing his testimony would help to legitimize your Senate trial which I know is of concern. You don't want to acquit based on a sham trial. That might look bad.
Sincerely,

P.S. Adam Schiff is a hero. He and the rest of the House management team are national heroes to a lot of people. Attacking Representative Schiff's meticulous work will backfire on you just as when you tried to discredit Lt. Col. Vindman. Dismissing and disparaging people who tell the truth is a favorite GOP tactic, but in the end, the GOP are the ones who appear as inadequate bullies. Just another bit of nonpartisan advice.

1-29-20

Dear Senator Johnson,

In listening to the impeachment trial's question and answer phase, I'm hearing a lot of questions by Republicans trying to ferret out a way to weasel out of their predicament. The short answer is this. Extortion is a crime. It's defined as "the crime of obtaining money or some other thing of value (in this case, investigations into a political rival) by the abuse of one's office or authority" (in this case, illegally holding back military aid mandated by Congress). In another dictionary, it's defined as "to obtain from a person by force, intimidation, or undue or illegal power."

Withholding evidence, in testimony or document form, constitutes obstruction and is a cover-up. "Obstruction of justice, in United States jurisdictions, is a crime consisting of obstructing prosecutors, investigators, or other government officials."(1) Both of these crimes have been committed by Trump. The predicament for Republicans is that an acquittal is obviously baseless no matter how you twist and evade and fabricate. Conviction is warranted.

Just think, somewhere out there is a Republican Party leader who wouldn't have to coerce the Party into staying with them.
Sincerely,

1) Wikipedia

1-30-20: Six national polls show Americans support having witnesses in the Senate impeachment trial by an average of 72.5%. (Poll results: CNN 69%, Quinnipiac 75%, Reuters 72%, Monmouth 80%, AP/NORC 68%, and WaPo 71%)

1-31-20

Dear Senator Johnson,
 More revelations have come out from Bolton's book manuscript, and Trump is running around calling him a liar. Again, it's easy to say whatever you want when you're not under oath. Trump puppet is the liar. All you have to do to figure this out is put Bolton under oath to testify in your trial. Override the obstruction. It's your job. Bolton may be a war hawk while I'm more of a dove, but he is not a liar or a traitor. He is a Republican who is NOT blinded by power, and for that, I applaud his willingness to stand upright on this matter.
 Your cover-up will eventually go up in flames if it hasn't already. Salvage yourself and hear witnesses and look at documents that were previously obstructed. Don't be beholden to Trump any longer. He isn't worth it.
Sincerely,

1-31-20: Marie Yovanovitch, former U.S. ambassador to Ukraine, retires from the State Department.

January 31, 2020

Dear Dr. Hallett,

Residents of the _____ area are invited to join me for a town hall meeting at 1:00pm on Sunday February 2, 2020 at _____ City Hall to discuss issues important to them.

In addition to my many town hall meetings, I am able to serve the constituents of the Fifth Congressional District in a variety of ways, including fulfilling flag and Presidential greetings requests, scheduling tours of Washington, D.C. and providing U.S. service academy nominations and student internships. You may see a full list of constituent services here.

To keep up-to-date on what is happening in Congress, you may also follow me on Facebook and Twitter.

*This mailbox is unattended. Please do not reply to this email.

Sincerely,

F. JAMES SENSENBRENNER, JR.
Member of Congress

TAMMY BALDWIN
WISCONSIN

United States Senate
WASHINGTON, DC 20510

1-31-20

COMMITTEES:
APPROPRIATIONS
COMMERCE
HEALTH, EDUCATION, LABOR, AND PENSIONS

Dear Dr. Hallett:

Thank you for contacting me about U.S. foreign policy toward Iran. I appreciate hearing from you.

I am always guided by the hard lessons that should be learned when America chooses to go to war in the Middle East. For years, many of us have been deeply concerned about President Trump stumbling into a war with Iran. After decades of U.S. military engagement in Middle East conflicts, Congress must not allow this administration to repeat the mistakes of the past.

The Constitution is very clear that only Congress has the authority to declare war. That is why I support Senator Tim Kaine's (D-VA) legislation to direct the removal of U.S. forces from hostilities against the Islamic Republic of Iran that have not been authorized by Congress (S. J. Res. 63). This bill requires that any hostilities with Iran must be explicitly approved by a declaration of war or specific authorization for use of military force (AUMF), but does not prevent the United States from defending itself from imminent attack. Additionally, I am a cosponsor of the No War Against Iran Act (S. 3159). Introduced by Senator Bernard Sanders (I-VT), this bill would prohibit the use of funds for any military force against Iran not explicitly authorized by Congress. The bill also clarifies that the 2001 AUMF, passed in response to the attacks on September 11, 2001, and the 2002 AUMF which authorized the invasion into Iraq, may not be construed to provide authorization for military actions against Iran.

President Trump's foreign policy towards Iran is a chaotic disaster that has not made us safer. I have consistently called for de-escalation and diplomacy to ease tensions with Iran, which is why I believe it was a mistake for President Trump to walk away from the Joint Comprehensive Plan of Action (JCPOA), that would have verifiably prevented Iran from acquiring a nuclear weapon. I support America using its leadership to work with the international community to maintain tough sanctions on Iran for its human rights violations, support for terrorism and criminal states like Assad's Syria, and its ballistic missile program. We have a constitutional responsibility to prevent the President from going to war with Iran and sending more American troops into harm's way without congressional authorization. We owe it to our service members and to the American people who are sick and tired of war in the Middle East. Rest assured, your thoughts will inform my views as the United States Senate exercises its role in American foreign policy.

Once again, thank you for contacting my office. It is important for me to hear from the people of Wisconsin on the issues, thoughts and concerns that matter most to you. If I can be of further assistance, please visit my website at www.baldwin.senate.gov for information on how to contact my office.

Sincerely,

Tammy Baldwin

Tammy Baldwin
United States Senator

1-31-20 evening: The Senate votes to forgo having any witness testimony or new documents allowed in their impeachment trial. Senator Baldwin (D-WI) voted in favor of witness testimony and document presentation. Senator Johnson (R-WI) voted against. Votes were along party lines except for two Republicans who voted with the Democrats. (Four Republican votes were needed in favor of witness testimony to have witnesses come before the Senate jury.)

1-31-20

Dear Senator Johnson,
    No witnesses, really? After you said that was the information you needed to assess the truth. You're acting out of fear of a vindictive president. Your lack of courage is astounding.
Sincerely,

2-1-20

Dear Senator Johnson,

    I still think it's quite clear from the evidence that you already have and are ignoring that Trump is guilty of the articles of impeachment and has thus shown himself to be an untrustworthy president. If a constituent can see it, why can't you? America doesn't want a hypocritical and underhanded president.

    You could still separate yourself from the cover-up by voting to convict. But then what? Trump and other GOP lemmings in Congress would ostracize you? It's the price you'd pay for voting on principle and defending our democracy. It's worth it if your conscience will then be at peace for the rest of your life. Don't underestimate a clear conscience.

Sincerely,

2-2-20: Representative Sensenbrenner held one of his Town Hall meetings in my locale. He has been good about holding these meetings to hear from his constituents through the years. I went to listen. Someone did ask about the impeachment. Basically, Representative Sensenbrenner felt the offenses weren't bad enough to be impeachable, and he prefers to have the decision whether or not Trump stays in office to be made at the national election in 9 months. I find this to be an odd, otherworldly stance designed to absolve oneself of any responsibility. I wonder what the presidential term threshold is to not be held accountable for illegal activity, 1 year, 18 months? It's hard to say.

2-3-20

Dear Senator Johnson,
    With regard to another partial argument being given by Trump's defense team that information exposing wrongdoing by a political candidate is relevant to the public, the catch is that you can't use taxpayer money congressionally mandated for military aid to a foreign country as leverage to get it. That's extortion and corruption.
    Representative Schiff and the House management team are saying that if a Democratic president committed the abuse and obstruction that Trump has committed, they too would be held accountable and removed from office.
Sincerely,

2-5-20

Dear Senator Johnson,
    Your cover-up is reminiscent of crime syndicate behavior. Everybody stick together even in the face of wrongdoing. Nobody break ranks for fear of losing their livelihood. You do realize that's how the Mob works, don't you? (Isn't the Mob often eventually brought down by tax fraud?)
    You have a president who is willing to allow foreign opinion and influence into our elections. By soliciting another country to perform an investigation into a political rival, he has shown he wants to use that country's opinion on past events if it would be to his advantage. A foreign country could very well give him what he wants in exchange for his favor, because America's favor is a big bargaining chip on the world's stage.
    If you vote to acquit, this is what you will be enabling (along with a number of other abuses, of course).
Sincerely,

Senator Johnson never did reply to any of these letters, probably because it would have been hard to defend his preordained position.

2-5-20: The Senate voted on whether or not to convict Trump for the articles of impeachment. On the 1st article, abuse of power, the vote count was 52 - 48 with "not guilty' in the majority. The vote was along party lines except for one Republican who courageously voted "guilty," Senator Romney of Utah. On the 2nd article of impeachment, obstruction of Congress, the vote count was 53 - 47 along party lines. Since a 2/3 majority was not reached for conviction, acquittal was granted. Senator Johnson (R-WI) voted "not guilty" on both articles, and Senator Baldwin (D-WI) voted "guilty" on both articles.

This is a true account that Trump would try to suppress. He calls any opinion that is critical of him "fake news." I tried to give my representative and senators in Congress an honest view of how their actions appear to a fair number of their constituents. Go out and vote. Our democracy depends on it.

Aftermath

2-7-20: Lieutenant Colonel Vindman was fired from the National Security Council by Trump. Vindman had testified before the House Impeachment Inquiry on 10-29-19. His twin brother, Lt. Col. Yevgeny Vindman, who also worked at the NSC was fired as well. Trump removed Gordon Sondland from his post as U.S. ambassador to the European Union.

2-19-20: Trump removed Acting Director of National Intelligence Admiral Joseph Maguire for allowing the House Intelligence Committee to be briefed on Russia's ongoing U.S. election interference which is partially aimed at helping Trump win re-election in November 2020.

3-1-20: The day after Joe Biden had a decisive win in the South Carolina Democratic primary election, Senator Johnson initiated an investigation into Hunter Biden's role on the board of Ukrainian energy company, Burisma. Senator Johnson has been in the Senate since 2011 which includes the entire time that Hunter Biden was on the Burisma board (4/2014 - 4/2019) during Joe Biden's vice presidency (1/20/09 - 1/20/17), and there was never any investigation brought forth then. Why now? Senator Johnson has succumbed to the same conspiracy theories that Trump uses to prop himself up.

March 2020: The COVID-19 pandemic surges in the U.S. Back in May of 2018, the Trump administration had dismantled the National Security Council's Global Health Security and Biodefense team which was responsible for pandemic preparedness. Trump failed to realize the implications of COVID-19 from the start and appeared only to take it more seriously when the stock market began to be affected. Even then, he persisted with disjointed, negligent, and reckless management of the crisis. His irresponsible lack of early testing and continued egregious shortfalls in testing for SARS-CoV-2 along with his negligent disregard for strategies proven to slow the transmission of the virus have and will cost lives.

Some say, "At least he did such and such," such as stopping non-U.S. citizens from entering the U.S. from China on January 31st. (Meanwhile, American citizens could return to the U.S. from China with recommendations for quarantine.) A president who does the very least is not performing up to the "standard of care" to use a medical legal term. One definition states that "standard of care refers to the degree of attentiveness, caution and prudence that a reasonable person in the circumstances would exercise. Failure to meet the standard is negligence, and the person who fails to meet the standard is liable for any damages caused by such negligence." Trump is not up to the standard of function that we need and expect from our national government. Let's find a president who truly comprehends how our well-being is connected to the rest of the world's.

4-3-20: Trump fired Michael Atkinson, the inspector general who notified Congress of the anonymous whistleblower complaint which told of Trump's pressure on Ukraine to investigate Joe Biden.

7-20-20: The United Nations Human Rights Council declared the U.S. assassination of Iran's General Soleimani during an official visit in Iraq unlawful under international law since the U.S. provided no evidence that an imminent threat existed at the time of the killing. The Trump administration withdrew from the U.N. Human Rights Council in June of 2018 citing an objection to the inclusion of other member countries with dubious human rights records.

The patterned list goes on.

Glossary of Personnel

Witnesses giving testimony mentioned in the letters in alphabetical order:
Dr. Fiona Hill – former senior director for Europe and Russia on the National Security Council from April 2017 to 7/19/19, succeeded by Tim Morrison
David Holmes – counselor for political affairs at the U.S. Embassy in Ukraine, testified to overhearing a phone call during a lunch in Kyiv between Ambassador Gordon Sondland and Trump involving Trump's wish to investigate political rivals
Tim Morrison – former senior director for Europe and Russia on the National Security Council from August 2019 until resigning a few months later on 10/31/19, recalled Sondland telling him that he (Sondland) had told a Ukrainian official that Ukraine's government would have to announce investigations into Trump's Democratic political foe to free up the U.S. military assistance. Also said Sondland told him there was no "quid pro quo," but that Ukraine needed to announce those investigations to get the aid.
Gordon Sondland – U.S. ambassador to the European Union 7/9/2018 – 2/7/2020, testified on October 17, 2019 in the impeachment inquiry and gave updated testimony on November 5, 2019 saying that there was a "quid pro quo"
William Taylor – acting U.S. ambassador to Ukraine from June 2019 to January 2020, succeeding Marie Yovanovitch. Taylor was

previously U.S. ambassador to Ukraine from 2006 to 2009. Testified during the House impeachment hearings on October 22, 2019.

    - His testimony transcript states that he "became increasingly concerned that our relationship with Ukraine was being fundamentally undermined by an irregular, informal channel of U.S. policymaking and by the withholding of vital security assistance for domestic political reasons."

Lt. Col. Alexander Vindman – National Security Council director for European Affairs, career U.S. Army officer – officially listened to July 25th phone call between Trump and Zelensky and also noted a July 10th meeting at the White House where Sondland told visiting Ukrainian officials that they would need to "deliver" before next steps (a meeting Zelensky wanted with Trump). On both occasions, Vindman said he took his concerns about the shifting Ukraine policy to the lead counsel at the NSC (National Security Council), John Eisenberg.

    -Both Williams and Vindman noted that the word "Burisma," a reference to the gas company in Ukraine where Hunter Biden served on the board, was used in the call but was missing from the rough transcript released by the White House.

Jennifer Williams – special advisor to the vice president for Europe and Russia, career State Department official in Vice President Mike Pence's office, one of the officials who listened in on the July 25th phone call.

Marie Yovanovitch – former U.S. ambassador to Ukraine, removed from her post by Trump in May 2019, succeeded by William Taylor

Other personnel mentioned in the book in alphabetical order:
Michael Atkinson, inspector general of the intelligence community, fired by Trump on 4/3/20
Tammy Baldwin, U.S. Senator, Democrat from Wisconsin, has been in office since 2013

Hunter Biden – son of Joe Biden and target of proposed investigation for time spent on board of Burisma, a Ukrainian gas company

Joe Biden – former vice president of the U.S. under President Barack Obama, candidate in Democratic primary for president in upcoming 2020 elections, target of proposed investigation for congressionally approved action of helping Ukraine remove a corrupt official when he was vice president

Robert Blair – senior advisor to acting White House Chief of Staff Mick Mulvaney. Blair was one of the officials who listened in on the July 25th phone call. He refused to testify during the House impeachment inquiry at his scheduled deposition because of the White House's direction not to appear.

John Bolton – former National Security Advisor in office from 4/9/18 until resigning on 9/10/19. Refused to testify during the House impeachment inquiry in November 2019, but then offered to testify in January 2020 during the Senate impeachment trial if he was subpoenaed. Oversaw the dismantling of the NSC's Global Health Security team in May of 2018.

Pat Cipollone – White House counsel

Michael Duffey – associate director of national security programs at the Office of Management and Budget (OMB), ordered by the White House to put a hold on the military aid for Ukraine. His involvement came to light on 12/21/19 in emails newly released after a Freedom of Information Act request.

John Eisenberg – National Security Council lead counsel

Rudy Giuliani – President Trump's personal attorney

GOP – Grand Old Party, nickname for the Republican Party

Lindsey Graham – U.S. Senator, Republican from South Carolina

Ron Johnson – U.S. Senator, Republican from Wisconsin, has been in office since 2011

Mitch McConnell – U.S. Senator, Republican from Kentucky, Senate Majority Leader

The Mueller Report – "Report on the Investigation into Russian Interference in the 2016 Presidential Election" by Special Counsel Robert S. Mueller, III. Redacted version released to the public by the U.S. Department of Justice on April 18, 2019.

Mick Mulvaney – acting White House chief of staff, involved in issuing Trump's order to withhold military aid from Ukraine, refused to cooperate with the House impeachment investigation

Devin Nunes – U.S. Representative, Republican from California, ranking member on the House Intelligence Committee. Met with Giuliani's associate, Parnas, multiple times and traveled to Europe to receive information on the progress of any investigations into the Bidens or information that might corroborate the debunked conspiracy theory that Ukraine interfered with the 2016 U.S. presidential elections instead of Russia.

Lev Parnas – worked with Rudy Giuliani in Ukraine to try to find information on the Bidens.

Nancy Pelosi – U.S. Representative, Democrat from California, Speaker of the U.S. House of Representatives

Adam Schiff – U.S. Representative, Democrat from California, House Intelligence Committee chair

Jim Sensenbrenner – U.S. Representative, Republican from Wisconsin, has been in office since 1979 and plans to retire at the end of his term in December 2020

Major General Qasem Soleimani – commander of Iran's Islamic Revolutionary Guard Corps' Quds Force

Donald Trump – U.S. President, impeached by the U.S. House of Representatives on 12/18/19, acquitted by the U.S. Senate on 2/5/20

Volodymyr Zelensky – Ukrainian President, elected in the spring of 2019 and assumed office on 5/20/19 during ongoing war with Russia which started in 2014

www.ingramcontent.com/pod-product-compliance
Lightning Source LLC
Chambersburg PA
CBHW051711090426
42736CB00013B/2643